Other Books in the WISDOMGAME
<u>How to Series:</u>

THE WORLD'S A FEAST

THE WORLD'S A FEAST

HELP YOURSELF!

Written by

Stephen Philip Means

WISDOMGAME®

Published 2009

WISDOMGAME

ISBN   978-0-9792448-1-0

DEDICATION

This manual is dedicated to all people who believe that dreams can come true, and who know they hold within themselves unlimited possibility.

TABLE OF CONTENTS

WISDOMGAME® <u>HOW TO SERIES</u>©

This manual is the first in a series of workbooks to help you help yourself.

<u>The World is a Feast</u>©.

You can easily help yourself. All you have to do is learn a few easy techniques, but you have to take action. Writing is a type of code that brings about what you have written about. This workbook asks you to take the simple action of writing down what you want. You are a very important person. You matter to those around you, and to the whole world. Write in this book. Draw in it. Cut it up. Digest it.

When you finish using this manual the objects, money, love, friendship, and joy you desire will begin appearing in your life as if by magic. The only requirement is that you actually use this workbook. If you read through it, you will increase your knowledge. This is good. If you fill in the blanks, write down your dreams and desires, and finish the exercises this will create a fantastic new world.

You deserve it. You are deeper than you know. You are a wonderful person.

YOU ARE UNLIMITED!

You are Unlimited.

How to use this workbook

The World is a Feast. Help Yourself! is specifically designed to be used for thirty days. You might be able to read through it quickly, and that's good. However, you will benefit much more, find your passion and obtain the friendship, love, abundance, and the objects you desire if you use this manual. Read it, contemplate the ideas, then write in it, draw in it, and chew it up.

Also keep this as a private journal. Don't share your desires with anyone, because that dilutes your power. Unlike information you may have studied in school, after you have digested this feast you will not have to throw it back up to pass an examination. In fact, for this workbook to be as successful as possible you must have the simple faith that it will work. And it will work, if you let nature take its course. It's a powerful set of instructions. You will receive all the things you desire.

This manual is designed around spiritual truths which have existed throughout time. These truths are listed on the left hand side of the page. Sometimes they are statements, and sometimes they are questions. A lined blank space is left below them for your personal notes. Fill in these spaces with your thoughts and answers to the questions and as you use the program,

"Understanding is the most powerful force we can create in ourselves"

.... Maurice Nicholl

Man develops on the side of knowledge and on the side of being.
Together this produces understanding.

as your ideas broaden, and as you become more attuned to what you desire, then go back and add more thoughts to what you have written. While the days progress, use the workbook and contemplate these ideas. Take your own time. Let the ideas sink in so they can take hold and start to work . . . but write in the manual. By writing you are taking action which will lead you to success.

Read and contemplate the left hand side of the page which is designed to change the way you are, that is, your being. Read the text on the right hand side of the manual and fill in certain areas. Make sure you do this.
Writing is a code that brings into reality what you have written. Please make a special effort to accomplish the tasks which are asked of you. They are easy and very simple but have an important result. In a direct way they move you toward obtaining what you want.

Many people in the past have started with very little and accomplished great deeds, had wonderful lives filled with friends and abundance. You are beginning a great adventure. You can have whatever you want. Always remember that if one person is capable of changing their circumstances and achieving greatness then you are too. The truth is the person that is reading this now is an unlimited person with great untapped resource. That resource is inside you. . .

The World's a Feast. Help Yourself!

Your level of being attracts your life.

How you are within your mind and your states of feeling magnetically attract others who have a like mind and like feeling states.

What do you think? _____

_____

_____

_____

INTRODUCTION

Helping yourself is lifting up your boots by your boot straps. Go ahead right now and try it. That's right, bend over, hold on to your shoes, and pick yourself up. It can't be done. You can't lift up your legs until you sit down. When you sit down you can pull up your feet and put them on the chair or bench, and then you can stand up. Helping yourself is a slow step by step process, sort of as if you were sitting in the bleachers, in the grand stand, slowly moving higher and higher by lifting up one leg after another, standing higher, sitting, pulling yourself up, standing and sitting as you move higher.

We want you to pull yourself up, to help yourself, but we don't want you to be in the grandstands. We want you to be part of the action. It's good if you enjoy watching others having fun, but the way humans learn is by doing. We get to know ourselves and the world around us by experiencing and participating in it. The word for this is "experiential." It means that as we experience life we become wise. This is **Wisdomgame®.** This book, '**The World's a Feast©,**' is the first in a series of ten books in the *Wisdomgame How to Series©,* published by **Wisdomgame®**. All the books in this series are experiential.

You can access our website at Wisdomgame.org, and there you can join our worldwide network. If you'd like to purchase our other books you can use the coupon at the back of this manual to mail in your order, or you can also order all our books at Wisdomgame.org . Each book is designed to stand on its own, but together you achieve a fantastic increase in ability and increase

Change your state of being and automatically change your life.

As you begin to think and create feelings of abundance, friendship, and love you attract people and objects like this.

_____

_____

_____

_____

of your potential. Within each book in this series, whenever possible, we use humorous stories. We believe that for whatever ills us, laughter is the best medicine.

These books are designed to entertain, educate, and enlighten. In starting this series you have taken a major step toward creating a life full of new, interesting, and exciting experiences. You are using a course of instructions which is easy and simple. As you participate you will experience easy changes and grow into a new you. Much like a river flows as it takes the path of least resistance, you flow into abundance, health, love, and fun. In this first series, **"The World's a Feast. Help Yourself!©"** you learn that the world is truly a feast, and you can easily have whatever you want.

HOW MUCH IS POSSIBLE?

The disciplines of neurology and psychology have studied human potential, and they tell us that human beings only use three or at the most four percent of their potential brain power. Mathematically, three percent divides into one hundred approximately thirty-three times, so if we are functioning at three percent, this means we have the capacity to be thirty-three times smarter, to be thirty-three times more efficient, and thirty-three times better.

Actually, as it turns out, the difference in using your brain at five percent compared to three percent is much more than a function of thirty-three. Using your brain at ten cent capacity qualifies you as a genius. The shift as you increase your brain power is tremendous. The fact is that no one knows the

21

If any area of you life is not working, one of your beliefs in that area needs to be changed.

Will you change?

_____

_____

_____

_____

extent of human potential, and no one knows how much that potential may increase.

> "I believe that there is no essential difference between what we call genius and everybody else except the so-called genius finds the correct way of using himself -- sometimes by fortunate circumstances, but more often than not by searching for it."

Moshe Feldenkrais

The Potent Self

This book is not particularly concerned with what potential future humans have, although speculation could be fun. Perhaps we will develop the power to influence matter, use x-ray vision, and to leap buildings with a single bound. Maybe we'll have big brains and communicate with thought waves. But right now, in this book, whether or not humans develop into super-beings doesn't much concern us. We aren't going to speculate on the possible evolution of man. For all we know humans may be de-evolving. There is an argument that movies and music on the radio are getting worse not better. That is, that the quality of life is deteriorating. Which may be humorous, but it is a moot question. In these lessons we're not concerned much about society; we care about you. We care about you, about helping you to help yourself.

Rather than resist a thought, simply place a thought of a higher nature by its side.

Simply replace the dim pictures in your mind with brighter ones.

_____

_____

_____

_____

WHAT THIS BOOK IS ABOUT

This book is about you. It is a record of your wants and desires, and how you are going to achieve them. As with all books in the family of how to books from **WISDOMGAME®,** it is important that you participate, because people learn by doing. This book is about you. You are getting to know yourself and finding out what you want and what your passions are.

Write in the book. Take time to fill in the following: This book is the property of:

_____.

If found please call: _____

_____.

Filling in the blanks is important. By doing this you will get to know what you really want and you will understand that you can help yourself. If you only read through this book, of course you will educate yourself. However, if you follow the step-by-step processes and participate with it you will know yourself, and when that happens you will be able to achieve whatever you want, and have fun doing it.

Ask and you will receive.
Seek and you will find.

Mathew 7:7

_____

_____

_____

_____

WHERE ARE YOU?

Everyone has a name, and everyone has a place to live. Even homeless people have a place -- though it may be in a car or the street. Not everyone is happy being where they are. Would you like to live in a newer apartment or home? Would you like to move? Where would you love to live? Fill in the following:

By this date _____, my place of living will look like this:

_____

_____

_____

_____

Congratulations! You have done very well. You have filled in the blanks above with a description of where you will be living and the date by which you will be living there. If you didn't fill in the blanks, that's okay.

Remember, writing is a type of code. It's a very powerful code which determines how the future turns out for you. When people learned to write, they began to plan their existence. They learned that putting thoughts down in words transformed those thoughts into reality. They changed their lives into a new reality by using words to describe their future reality.

In years to come you may look back at your descriptions and have a laugh. One of the first sayings of Taoism, from the old man Lao Tse, goes like this:

**To reach the goals you've set for yourself,
be the person you want to be.**

Who do you want to be?

_____

_____

_____

_____

When the man of supreme wisdom first hears of the Way, he immediately searches out a real person and begins his study. When the man of higher wisdom hears of the Way, he finds all the books he can and studies them all. When the man of knowledge hears of the Way, he reads about it. When the average man hears of the Way, he laughs. If he didn't laugh, it wouldn't be the Way.

When you have finished **The World's a Feast!©** and you look back, you will laugh because now you are living in a much nicer place. You will have money, a new car, and a home, love or whatever you want and your life will be interesting, exciting, and fun. When you finish this book, you will help yourself to what you want.

THE WORLD IS A FEAST

This workbook is not suggesting you do anything illegal, dishonest, unethical or immoral. We know you wouldn't do that. Anyway, none of that is necessary. A couple of short tales of wisdom. . . called aphorisms . . . may help you understand yourself.

Once, a couple went to their friends' wedding. It was a gala affair. After the marriage, everyone gathered in a great hall where there was a red carpet, and flowers, and a great feast. Although the couple was hungry, they didn't fill their plates for fear that the old uncle, the relatives, or the married couple themselves would see and think they were pigs. They were hungry. There was plenty food for everyone, but they only took meager portions. When the

The Universe handles the details.

Allowing the infinite intelligence of the Universe to figure out how to bring to you your desires means to trust that you will be fulfilled.

_____

_____

_____

_____

wedding was over, the poor couple went home to bare cupboards and ate cereal.

"Why didn't we eat more?" asked the husband.

"What?!" replied the wife, "And let all the relatives see we were hungry."

"But Uncle Fred is rich, and he ate like a pig. Did you see all the food on his plate?"

"He's rich. He can do that. We're poor. We'll never have enough."

Actually, the world is a feast. There is a hot, sweet smelling pie waiting for you on the window sill. You don't have to tip-toe around and sneak it away. It's yours. It was baked for you.

All you want is out there for the taking and this workbook,

The World's a Feast!

Help Yourself ©

by

WISDOMGAME®

Is going to show you the way!

JUST DO IT!

Not only don't people take advantage of what is offered to them for free, but they also make mountains out of molehills. Grant McStone, the owner of a New York City construction company, tells this story:

The level of success you attain matches your dreams.

Those who succeed have a clear and focused picture of their success.

_____

_____

_____

_____

"When I was a kid out on the farm we had a pile of cow you-know-what. Over the years it had grown to a giant pile and it smelled pretty bad. We stared at it day after day thinking how much of a job it was and how hard it was going to be to get rid of it. Days turned into weeks and months into years. Meanwhile, it kept on growing bigger. Why, we probably spent more than a couple of years just thinking about it. Finally, Dad says, "I've had it." So we get the truck and shovels. In about four hours we got that danged manure moved and spread out over the back forty. Four years of thinking about it and half a day of doing it, not to mention the stink."

WHAT'S THE POINT?

As we grow, all parts of our bodies fall into habit. We learn to talk with certain vocal sounds, and as we talk we move our hands in particular ways. When we walk, our bodies have a characteristic gait. We use our eye muscles with repeated motions. What we do and see is controlled by habit. We develop fixed muscular patterns which are ways of receiving and giving out communication. Often, because we've become fixed in our habits, we're like the couple at the wedding who didn't understand it was okay to simply take as much as they desired. We see and understand our world as limited because our own habits tell us the place we live in is a limited world. In fact, we have grown accustomed to seeing lack. Abundance sits right in front of us, but we can't see it because the habitual way we look and see limits us.

The world is only as limited as we make it. Often, we imagine obstacles

The Universe supports itself by encouraging each of us to fully and freely express our talents.

In order to have a life that works perfectly, each of us must be doing what we were created to do.

_____

_____

_____

_____

to be bigger than they are. How many times have you thought like Grant McStone? Have you ever gotten so exhausted just thinking about how a big a job lay ahead that you didn't even start the job? An old Chinese proverb states "A journey of a thousand miles begins with one step." Really, it should read like this:

"The end of the thousand mile journey begins with the first step."

In truth what is important is neither the beginning nor the end of the trip, but rather enjoying and appreciating the moments of the journey. Yet, if you never take the first step, if you never begin, if you never start to live, you may feel as if you had always lived in a dream. If you're not experiencing the wealth, health, love, and fun you want -- then there is a journey ahead of you. Right now, it may look much bigger than it is. It's not big. It's easy and it's fun. The journey ahead of you is to help yourself.

Remember, to pull yourself up by your bootstraps you have to sit down first, lift one foot, then the next so you can stand on the next level.

Right now, sit down. That is, take a break and think about what you want. This is the first step.

What's the first thing you do when you find yourself in a hole?

You stop digging!

Take a break, sit down and think about what you want.

35

When we define our purpose, anything that happens to us appears more meaningful.

Our purpose provides us with our general connection to the Universe. It establishes us as part of the larger picture.

_____

_____

_____

_____

To get what you want, you have to want. You can't think that it would be *nice* to have wealth, health, and so on. You especially won't get the "so on" if you think *maybe you could have it*. You need to be specific. If you want a million dollars, you can't get that if you want "money." If you want to own a five-bedroom-three-bath home, you can't get that if you want "a place to live." If you want a fantastic lover, you won't get that if you just want a "mate." You have to be specific. What do you want?

You have to be specific, and you can't be bland. You can't be tepid. You need passion! You need to energize your desires and imagine them as real. You must have wants that have color, smell, sensation, taste and feeling. With your desires you must create images in your mind that replicate reality, and you must desire them with the passions of your heart. This begins with a wish and a challenge.

MAKE YOUR WISH

It's okay to wish. Wishing is dreaming and change begins in dreaming. Write fast, don't think, and don't censor yourself, write

I wish _____

_____

_____

and some items that I wish I owned are:

1. _____

2. _____

The only way to improve your life is to conceive of a better one.

Once you conceive of it, then make believe it is real. Cultivate it, nourish it, and it will fill your life with its presence.

_____

_____

_____

_____

3. _____

4. _____

I wish I was _____

_____

I wish I had _____

_____

I wish I could _____

_____

I am free to have as much as I want. I wish for more and I write it down:

I wish for _____

plus _____

plus _____

plus _____

There is no limit on me or my wishes.

I wish for _____

and _____

and _____

The life force is eternal and universal and limitless.

We all have within us Unlimited Power.

_____

_____

_____

_____

THE CHALLENGE OF WISHING

Take a dare. We dare you to consider your problems as challenges. Whatever the problem, if you consider it a challenge then you meet it head on. You can get behind a challenge, it will energize you. A problem is heavy. A challenge is positive and lighter. Now, the problem of "wishing" is that it is a very weak mode of expressing what you want. Here's the challenge: change that weak "wish" into a positive statement of desire.

"I wish I was a rock star." "I wish I had a million dollars." "I wish I had a new house." "I wish I was smarter." These statements show how weak is a *wish* statement. If you want a cup of coffee, you say "I'm going to have a cup of coffee." Usually, unless you're out of coffee, you don't wish for it. You just go get it. Wishing is sort of a statement of lack. It is a very, very weak statement. Look at the difference in these statements. "I wish I were a rock star." "I want to be a rock star." "I have to be a rock star." "I've got to be a rock star." Which is stronger?

"Wish" is very cool. "Want" warms up a bit. "Have to" is getting hot. "Got to" means you are burning hot. When you have "got to," you are under a compulsion to get it done. Where does the compulsion come from?

You make it up! Because you want it, and because you burn red hot and

Your wishes are fulfilled right now.

The unlimited forces of the Universe know your wishes and they are beginning to manifest into reality at this very moment.

_____

_____

_____

_____

have passion, it will happen. Now, go back to all your wishes on the previous pages and pick out two special wishes. Change your "wishing" language first to "having to have" and then to "got to have."

First wish:

I have to have _____

_____

Change to:

I've got to have _____

_____ .

Second Wish:

I have to have _____

_____

and

_____ .

Change to:

I've got to have _____

_____ ,

And _____ .

"No one has plumbed the depths of the human mind."
Ernst Holmes

Focus on the half of the glass that is full.

> **When you focus on your dream and how it can be fulfilled, you discover everything you need to create the life of your dreams.**

_____

_____

_____

_____

The Leap of Faith

The unconscious mind is like a giant iceberg with the majority of its contents under the surface of the conscious mind. (order: **You are Unlimited. How to Use Unconscious Forces©** from **WISDOMGAME®**) This iceberg will respond to requests from your conscious mind and, over time, direct you to what you want. The trick to using your unconscious forces is to make requests *as if* they were actually true. Instead of saying "I want to own a new house" or "I want to have a new love affair," or whatever . . . change those statements to read *as if* they were already in existence, *as if* they were already true. Use the present tense and say, "I own a new car"; "I am in a new love affair."

Now, go back to your wish list or your statements of "want to" and "got to" and change them to the present tense, *as if* you had them already. Fill them in and fill up this page. Write this down: **I own and already have . . .**

1. I own and already have

_____

_____.

2. I own and already have _____

_____

_____.

3. I own and already have _____

_____.

45

Flow with the current. Know that whatever happens it is for your own good.

Be prepared. Be alert to opportunities. Your success is just around the corner.

_____

_____

_____

_____

I own and already have:

4. I own and already have _____

_____

_____.

Good! Again we repeat -- you will experience change in your life to the extent that you actually do the exercises and fill in the blank spaces.

Trying and Doing

There is a big difference between trying and actually doing. As an experiment, set a glass of water or a cup of coffee in front of you. Now, *try* to pick it up. Don't actually pick it up. . . only *try* to lift it. The act of "trying" is moving out and stopping half way, being frozen, or in some way or manner subverting the successful attempt. When you succeed in an act you don't *try*. You actually do it. This may sound like semantics -- that is, using words to make a point -- but it's an important point. Next time you hear one of your acquaintances say "I'll try to come over," you'll know just that. They will try and somehow they will subvert their attempt to come over, and they won't be there. A successful statement is "I'll do it." When you hear "I'll try. . . ," it means "I'll try . . . but I won't be successful." If you are *trying to help yourself*, stop trying and **start doing.**

You are a wonderful person. You can help yourself!

Go back to the previous pages and look at them. Did you "try" to fill in the

47

Imagine one year and then five years from now. What's your life going to be like?

As the pictures you see become clearer, the reality is approaching.

_____

_____

_____

_____

blanks, or did you fill in the blanks? If this is too much work for you just think how much work it's going to be hauling those bags of cash to the bank, or living in your beautiful new home, or kissing your new lover. If you *try* to have those things, you'll never have them. You have to

Grab life by the ass and drag it to you!

DRAWING PICTURES

We made the above statement very visual for a distinct purpose. The more colorful you paint your wishes, desires, and wants the more quickly they happen. Which picture is more vivid: 'The sky was full of clouds,' or 'The blue sky was filled with white clouds.' Obviously, the more you festoon the statements of your wishes, desires, and wants the more they impress. The more impression they make on you and the world, the quicker they come into reality. By adding colors, sounds, tastes and feelings to your statements they quickly manifest in reality.

This book is **The World's a Feast!**© It is not a book to teach you to be creative. **WISDOMGAME®** publishes a workbook designed to develop human creative potential by helping you complete your creative project. (please order **MANUAL TO BRING HEAVEN TO EARTH** © published by **WISDOMGAME®.**)

Continue. . . . you are now creating the world you desire.

49

There is an abundance of health, happiness, and prosperity for everyone.

Your source of supply does not depend on anyone but yourself.

_____

_____

_____

_____

It is important to paint vivid pictures. By adding color, sounds, tastes, smells, and feelings to your wishes, wants, and desires you give them three-dimensional plasticity. That is, you form them in your mental substance. As they become real there, and you give them qualities and feelings, they begin to emerge into reality. Soon, and indeed sooner than you think, they are realities.

THOUGHTS ARE REAL

Pictures you form in your mind have a real existence of about a mille-second. That is why you need to review them over and over and add layers of colors, sounds, smells, tastes and sensations. If you are longing for an expensive new car you will be thinking of the color, perhaps the sound of the door slamming shut, the smell of the leather, the taste of caviar, and the sensation of speeding. . . . whatever you associate with the purchase of a new vehicle. You will of course experience the feelings of success and accomplishment whenever you complete any of Wisdomgame's® **How to Series.**©

Once you have decided on what you want it becomes necessary to picture that object as real, to re-picture it, and re-picture it until in your imagination you can taste, touch, see, smell and feel it. As it begins to exist in your imagination, it will soon be born in your reality. But you can't just think about it. You've got to make it real. This is done through feelings.

You mind does its building by the power of your thought.

> Your life's creations take form in exact accord with your mental image,
> and desire builds the mental image for you.

_____

_____

_____

_____

WANT IS AN EMOTION

Where is desire located? If you're hungry, obviously that is located in the physical body, in your stomach. If you "ought" to eat, that's a thought and is located in your mind. If you don't have hunger pangs, but you want to eat, what is that? That's a wish, want, or desire, and as such it's classified as an emotion. Emotions are tied to breathing, and breathing correctly is a very important art. But pictures in your mind, no matter how plastic, will never become real until those pictures produce white-hot feelings (emotions).

Making Life Real

The purpose of **How to Help Yourself ©** by **WISDOMGAME®** is to show you that you can help yourself. It is important to us that you awaken to your full potential as a human being. **WISDOMGAME®** offers you a wide variety of books on many subjects, and we hope that through studying these subjects you will experience life in the greatest way possible.

We weren't born to experience our existence as if we were in a fuzzy cotton ball. Sometimes life is hard. Sometimes it's full of joy, and sometimes our experiences can transcend even our ability to communicate our experiences. Life is a mystery, but it shouldn't be lived as if it were a dream. It is indeed possible to have everything that you want. The only cost is that you have to learn some simple techniques and then apply yourself.

Learning is the joyous never-ending process of getting to know yourself. Whatever age and place you are at this very moment is the place to begin.

Doing what we love is our way of supporting the Universe.

The Universe in turn gives us total support and encourages us to
continue to support it.

_____

_____

_____

_____

You can learn right now that life is abundant and fun.

You have done well. You are a great person. You can have whatever you want. You deserve it. The world is a feast filled with riches, friendship, and love, and it is available to anyone who believes they can have it.

You are unlimited!

The more you expand your thinking, the ability to create your dreams will also expand.

> **As you expand the horizon of your imagination you open the doorway to abundance.**

_____

_____

_____

_____

CHAPTER 1

FINDING OUT WHAT YOU WANT

Not everyone knows exactly what they want, and although many people have a general idea of what they want, it is difficult for them to form a direction. People move along from day to day like sailboats on calm seas, thinking they are moving toward a goal but in reality they are drifting, going nowhere. What do you have to do to find a direction and start moving in that direction?

If we stay with the analogy of a sailing boat, we discover an interesting point in our dictionary as it defines the verb form of the word 'list.' On a ship, "to list" is to lean over to one side. On the sailboat of your life, are you leaning to one side: are you taking on water? Are you sinking? Have you started to list?

If you're taking on water and the boat of your life is starting to list, it's time to use the problem to solve the problem. It's time to start a list.

The noun form of 'list' is defined as "a series of names, items, figures written or printed." Further, the dictionary defines the term "enter the lists," as to "make or accept a challenge." In **The World's a Feast!©,** published by **WISDOMGAME®,** we change problems to challenges. Lack of direction is not a problem; it is a challenge. In fact, our direction in life is determined as we conquer our challenges. You can easily conquer your challenges.

The most important action you can take is to write out a plan.

Your plan reminds your subconscious mind that this is your desire, and
your subconscious mind begins to work on it.

_____

_____

_____

_____

ENTER THE LISTS

My biggest problem is _____

_____.

My second most pressing problem is _____

_____.

Mt third most important problem is _____

_____.

THE TRUTH

The truth will set you free, and while truth is varied and different for different people, there is one truth that everyone shares: We are all going to die. Although this seems a little blunt, it is the absolute truth. If you focus on this truth, soon instead of being depressed, you will rise out of the doldrums. The fact that someday you won't be here anymore is a real truth. Sometime, sooner or later, you're going to be gone. It's nothing to worry about. Rather, celebrate because you are here and there is still time to do what you want. It is said, people don't regret what they did. The things you don't do you regret most.

Hey! Let's not have regrets. If you don't have the life you want, it's time to go out and get a new one. You have to take that trip, write that book, start playing guitar, tell your relatives and friends that you love them. If you don't,

Time is an illusion

Tomorrow at this time, the time will still be now. To start, you always start now.

_____

_____

_____

_____

is your life going to be any different tomorrow? What time is it **now?** In twenty four hours it will be exactly that time again. In fact, **the time is always now.** The time to start living is always **now**.

If you imagine a big black raven sitting on your shoulder, it will always whisper "**do it now**." The raven is Death. It's not being morbid. It's enlightened, and it is telling you to take the first steps on your journey. Time is running out. You don't have time to drift on the sea anymore. The ship is taking on water. You're starting to list.

WHY MAKE LISTS

A lot of people hate lists. They consider them to be a chore, something that's beneath them. Perhaps they think they are perfect. At one time they made lists of everything. But now, they don't need them. Either the lists didn't work, or they worked so well that now, they don't need them. But lists are always an important part of overcoming challenges. They are an important part of your personal change.

If it's going, it's going to go wrong.

Murphy

Murphy's law states that whatever can go wrong, probably will go wrong. Chaos, that is, disorder, is almost a natural outcome of being human. We are, by nature, hunters and gatherers. Nowadays, very few are hunters and most make an art of gathering clutter, junk and too much stuff. It's a national disease. Yet, somehow, not everyone sinks under the weight of that disorder.

Inside your mind say "Yes!" to every one of your intentions.

When you write out a plan you are giving intention to your thoughts.

_____

_____

_____

_____

They list, and then they right themselves. Listing clears disorder.

Right now, you can determine if you need to make lists. Think about your home or look around at your environment. What's it like? Is it organized? How about your bookcase? Are the books in order? What's your paperwork like? What does the inside of your car look like? How neat and clean is your living space? Is there a project you need to work on? Is your mind organized? If what you see around you is disorganized, then more than likely what you have inside your head is also disorganized. Can you see how there is an interplay between your inside world and the outside world? Do you see that the inside affects the outside, and what's on the outside conditions what's going on inside your head.

You can get organized. It's not difficult.

HOW TO GET ORGANIZED

Take all your paperwork, or whatever is cluttering your space, and pile it in a big stack. Make two piles. One pile will be a "save" pile. The other will be a "throw away" pile which goes in the trash. Throw away all envelopes, wrappers, advertisements, dated materials, junk, useless receipts, and stuff you don't want. When you finish, take out the trash and throw it away. Don't look back.

If you don't have a **hanging file system,** go and get one. Make one file called 'immediate action' and leave it out. Sort out the rest of the paperwork

The trick is to keep your eye on the goal.

Use daily, weekly, monthly and yearly goal lists. Look at them every day.
You will succeed!

_____

_____

_____

_____

into individual files, and order your files alphabetically and put them in your hanging file. Clean up your house. Do your laundry. Clean your car, and do whatever it takes to give you the feeling of being ordered. Structure your life around these ordering chores until it becomes a way of life.

"Easier said than done," you might reply.

"Remember Grant McStone. Just do it!"

A supporter of **WISDOMGAME®,** Dr. Rod Nee, was good at giving advice, but not at following it. As a proponent of Zen and Tibetan Buddhism he pointed to the moon and said,

> **"You can make the place where you meditate a simple paradise with one flower, one stick of incense, or one candle. You can transform the most ordinary of rooms into an intimate sacred space, into an environment where everyday you come to the meeting with your true self with all the joy and happy ceremony of one old friend greeting another."**

However, in his old age, curiosity and attachment got the better of Dr. Nee. He began to visit thrift stores where he gathered a splendid collection of worthless junk. He couldn't throw anything away, and soon the only way to circumnavigate his living space was to tiptoe gingerly on small trails between his books, stacked papers, and curios.

The **other** will never visit Dr. Rod Nee.

THE OTHER

The 'other' is a mysterious concept which is hard to explain. However, in this series **How to Help Yourself©** by **WISDOMGAME®,** we don't shy away from difficulty. In fact, it is our challenge to present the truth to you no

Passion is bliss.

> To be wholly absorbed in the joy of doing what you love is bliss.

_____

_____

_____

_____

matter how obtuse, arcane, or difficult the subject, is and/or how foolish we may appear.

Life is beautiful and mysterious. The fact that we are alive and conscious is an enigma. It is something quite difficult to understand. We accept that we are communicating when we have an idea in our heads, make a vibration in the air and somehow that idea appears in someone's head. Reality, existence, communication: These are, in fact, truly mysterious concepts. The way we define ourselves, how we move in our environment, and our existence as humans and as animals -- these are also mysterious concepts. The 'other' is beyond these.

Phenomena are the experiences of our existence. For instance, a wind-storm is a phenomenon. The **'other'** is a word used to describe a reality which exists outside phenomenon. Ordinarily, for instance, we might think of this as visions of Jesus or Buddha, seeing interlaced rainbows, visitations from dead loved ones, spontaneous healings, and precognition. However, to describe the 'other' like this is similar to describing the smell of a rose by saying it's kind of like a geranium. They are in fact both fragrances but quite different.

The 'other' is something new which is constantly changing and varied and can't be directly experienced, but it does exist. It is difficult to define, but one way that this 'other' can enter you is as a form of lust for life or **passion** . . . which is individual and new for each person. No one knows exactly where it comes from or how it enters, but when it does, your problems and challenges pale in comparison to your energy and ability to overcome them.

The whole Universe is similar to a clockwork with all its wheels in mesh and moving together.

And so are you. That which is above is also that which is below.

_____

_____

_____

_____

Passion enters mysteriously. There is nothing you can do to request it or command it to appear. All a person can do, so to speak, is to open the window and let in the breeze. Once you clean out the junk from your mind and your physical place, as you order your interior and exterior environment, a space is created for the other, the passion, to enter. It won't enter a disorganized home, there's too much to get in its way.

THE OPEN WINDOW

In Hebrew the name of God is Yod He Vau He. Roughly, in English these Hebrew words translated to "The creative hand opens the window looking in to the window looking out."

You have already opened the window to allow passion to join your life. When you "Entered the Lists" on the previous pages you accepted the challenge that you could find solutions to your problems. You "listed" your three biggest problems. Amazing as it seems, **the solution to these problems is contained within the problems**. This is using the problem to solve the problem. Inside your problems, exactly as you have worded them, is the key to solving those problems.

S. P. D. King, well known Indianapolis racer, was asked about the secret that made him successful. He replied, "It's no secret. It's just that the average Joe, and even the most experienced drivers always seem to use the brakes too much in the curves. If you want to be a great driver, you have to use the

Every problem is an outward manifestation of our state of consciousness.

By changing problems to challenges and overcoming them, we clear our consciousness, and the problems disappear.

_____

_____

_____

_____

curves themselves. Make a slow approach to a curve, but then give it all you've got and accelerate out of them. You got to use the curves."

You use the same technique when approaching your problems. First you make a slow approach. Take a break, sit down, look at your problems, separate them, write them out, think them over, change them to challenges, and list them. After that, you're into the curve, and you need to accelerate and use the problem to solve the problem.

Note: If you are reading through this book, that's great! However, you will pretty much stay the same. If you write in this book, and fill in the blanks, you will know yourself. You will appreciate the change. **If you haven't yet listed your problems, go back a few pages and write them down.**

Now, go back to the listings of your problems as challenges and read them.

Okay, rewrite the problem to be the solution:

Write the problem as the solution:

My biggest solution is _____

_____.

My second most pressing solution is _____

_____.

My third most important solution is _____

_____.

The map is not the territory.

You are much bigger than you understand you to be. You are deeper.
You have more ability. You can do more, have more and be more. You
are at the trailhead of uncharted territory: You.

_____

_____

_____

_____

Another note: Do you need to know how an internal combustion engine works to be able to drive a car? Or do you need to know how electricity flows before you turn on the lights?

Most people can drive a car, but they don't know much about engines. The key to solving your problems is to change the problems to solutions. You don't need to know how this works to make it work. It has a name. It's called reframing.

REFRAMING

The problem presents its solution. That is, held within the challenge is the solution to the problem. Here are some examples:

Jack B. Uilder, a mason, lived with his family in a house with a flat roof. A rainstorm was coming and Jack didn't have enough time to get a roofer in to fix the leaks, so Jack bought some thick polyvinyl plastic and covered the roof by tacking it down to the fascia. The rain beat heavy that night, but the plastic held. There were no leaks.

During the next week Jim was pretty happy the water left on the roof didn't leak and evaporated. but later the wind picked up and started blowing hard. Even though he had weighted down the plastic with bricks and tacked it to the fascia, the plastic started to lift up. Soon, it would be torn. All that work was to be ruined, and another rainstorm was just around the corner. What to do?

Jim turned on the water and took the hose to the top of the roof. The plastic

73

Locked in every problem is the solution to the problem.

> **If any area of your life is not working you need to change your beliefs about it. There is a solution to every problem if you look.**

_____

_____

_____

_____

hadn't leaked in the previous rain. So when he sprayed the water on the roof, the weight of the water on the plastic sitting on the flat roof held it down. Soon, the wind died down and the winter rains came and went, and the Uilders were able to get a new roof that spring. Jim understood that held within his problem was the answer to his problem.

Now, Jim's niece wasn't great looking, but she wasn't bad looking either. She was a nice girl, but she just couldn't find the right man. She didn't know what to do. She didn't know she could find help from **WISDOMGAME®** (Order **HOW TO FASCINATE the OPPOSITE SEX©.**)

She didn't know what to do and was lonely most of the time. She went to bars and bookstores and the library and the market. No luck! She tried dances and her church and parties. Still no luck. Poor Jane!

All the men seemed like duds with beer in their stomachs and football on their minds. Then she talked to her uncle Jim. He told her about his roof and how he used the water to weight the plastic, and how he used the problem to cure the problem. He told her to put this ad in the paper:

"Plain Jane needs a makeover. Fix my hair. Do my face. Help me buy new outfits. I need a coach and I'm willing to pay."

An unemployed male hair stylist read her ad, came over, and did her hair. They went shopping and enjoyed each other's company. Pretty soon the relationship bloomed. They fell in love, got married, and lived a beautiful

One dollar, ten dollars, a hundred dollars, a thousand dollars, ten thousand dollars, one hundred thousand dollars, one million dollars comes to me easily and without much effort.

Because I support the Universe, the Universe supports me in everything.

_____

_____

_____

_____

life. The challenge held the solution to the problem.

To '**reframe**' means to look at your life's pictures without the strangling emotions normally attached to difficult situations. For instance, previously, you may have written "I need money; I want money; I've got to have money." You may be approaching this curve of needing money with apprehension and a feeling that this is going to be difficult. The "curve of life" is throwing you fear and doubt.

Now, let's look at your problems and reframe them. Fill in the following.

I need _____ and it **comes to me naturally and with ease.**

And more:

I need _____

And it comes **naturally and with ease.**

I need _____

And it comes **naturally and with ease.**

There doesn't have to be fear or apprehension attached to any picture you create about your life. The emotions of fear and apprehension cause a fight or flight reaction with adrenaline which speeds your heart. But what you want to do when life throws you a curve is slow down into the curve and then accelerate with excitement toward your goal. Excitement is beneficial when it is directed toward fulfilling a positive picture you have created.

**The emotionally colored picture which you hold in your mind
is the cause of the life the artist (you) experiences.**

> **There is no lack in the Universe. Its substance is abundance. You use this substance to draw to you a wonderful life.**

_____

_____

_____

_____

To use the curve your problems present, first you slow down, look at your problems as challenges, then use that to create excitement toward solving those challenges.

REPAINT YOUR PICTURES

In the following section you are going to take a quick look back over all your wishes, wants, desires, problems and solutions, and then use the empty spaces to repaint those pictures. You will make all the problems more vivid and then redraw them brighter and bolder as if you had solved them already. This will reframe them as solutions.

For instance, if you said "I need a new lover," now you will write: 'I easily get along with others and right now I discover a man (a woman) and we move naturally into a relationship.' If you wrote 'I need a new house,' now you will write, 'Ral estate is fun. I enjoy looking for a new place. My new home comes easily to me.' And so on.

Okay, go back to where you listed your problems as solutions, read them over, and reframe them below in the present tense as accomplished in a simple, easy, natural manner.

1. _____

_____.

"If the artist be priest of beauty, nevertheless this beauty is to be sought only according to the principle of inner need, and can be measured only according to the size and intensity of the need."

. . . Wassily Kandinsky

How intense is your desire?

_____

_____

_____

_____

2. _____

_____.

3 _____

_____.

Now add colors, tastes, feelings, and sensations. Make these descriptions simple, easy, and vivid. Remember, the pictures you paint of the future will come true when you vividly paint them and fill them with positive feelings. If the pictures you paint are dull, your life will be dull. If the pictures you paint are bright, your life will be enlivened. Take some time right now and redo the pictures you have drawn.

Three important solutions now enliven my future, and as I paint them they easily come alive with colors and sounds and sensations:

The colorful solutions to my problems are:

1. _____

_____

_____

_____

_____.

2. _____

_____

"No one has ever plumbed the depths of either the conscious or the subjective life. In both directions we reach out to infinity."

. . . Ernest Holmes

You are Unlimited!

_____

_____

_____

_____

3._____

_____

_____.

Keep going. You're unlimited.

4. _____

_____

_____

_____

_____.

Now, below draw a picture of a smiling face with stars in the eyes. It's you, because everything you want is now flowing to you easily and without much effort.

Keep going. You are helping yourself.

From the time we are babies until the time we die everyone craves attention.

The price you pay for friendship is your attention to your friends.

_____

_____

_____

_____

Chapter 2

LEARNING HOW TO LEARN

You are learning **HOW TO HELP YOURSELF.** You are getting to know who you are. Whenever you like, because you have written in this book, you can look back to see where you have been. You will understand when you look back that you are changing and change is natural to being human. This is the beginning of learning how to learn, and to learn about yourself is a wonderful experience which makes you a talented person. (Order: *How to* **LEARN HOW TO LEARN© by WISDOMGAME®)** To fully develop your talents, while it seems almost paradoxical, you need to know what you don't know. How can you know what you don't know? Is that possible? What do you think?

Fill in the following:

I don't understand _____

_____.

What does it mean to _____

_____?

I wonder _____

_____.

Scientists agree that humans use between three and ten percent of their brains.

> **Anyone who uses ten percent of their brain power is considered a genius.**

_____

_____

_____

_____

Most of us were so busy as children being forced into the boxes of our parents that we never learned how to learn. Have you ever thought about how you think? Not 'what you think, but *'how'* you think?' Have you ever examined *how you learn*?

This is not a trick question that won't be on next week's quiz, but *when did you quit learning?* It's not a trick question, because the answer is: "Humans never quit learning." However, the ability to learn quickly is different. **WISDOMGAME®** can read minds. We know how you're doing:

You are fantastic!

You are really a fantastic person. **WISDOMGAME®** is very happy you are filling in the blanks, getting to know who you are and solving your problems. Please continue. The world is a big and beautiful place full of opportunity for everyone. It really is a wedding feast. It's fun. Passion can enter you life, and if you want you can have it all. The World is a Feast. You can **Help Yourself.**

A UNIVERSAL PRINCIPLE

Everyone is different and the truth itself is ever-changing. The future is not something that is already established, but rather at this very moment we create, fill and fulfill patterns we have brought forward from earlier moments. As we move into the future, we create, fill and fulfill the future. How does time appear to you?

Time is _____

_____.

What you place your attention on increases.

If you attend to good, the good increases. If you think about abundance, abundance increases. What are you attending to today?

_____

_____

_____

_____

Does the past exist? Are your ancestors living in another time and space? Does the future already exist? Are we simply moving in to it and living through it? Is time a continuum? Is time travel possible? What time is it?

The clock says it's _____.

Whatever your clock time, the time is always **now.** Now is always present. Now is when you must begin. In truth, it is the only time there is. The way you use thoughts, things, and people, <u>right now</u> is how you are going to **Help Yourself.** Although the future is not fixed, there is a principle which works. Now, here it is:

What you place your attention on increases.

This principle works in the positive and in the negative. Your attention is what fills the pattern you create as you move into the future. If you put your attention on increase, you will find increase. If you put your attention on lack, you will fill that pattern and increase your lack.

Sally Johnson was always worried about money. When she went shopping she would look at price tags and say to herself, "This is just too, too expensive. I can't afford this." Eventually she bought all her clothes at thrift shops. Pretty soon she ended up on the street eating out of trash cans. In one of the trash cans she found inspiration. Someone had accidentally thrown away a copy of **The World is a Feast©.** Sally also found a couple of apples and one half a sandwich. As she was eating lunch she played Wisdomgame®

Attitude is everything.

When we evaluate or judge anything we stop the flow of energy through
us. Experience the inherent perfection of everything. . . including
yourself.

_____

_____

_____

_____

and filled in the blanks and **got to know herself**. She understood **attitude is everything,** and from that moment on she was **positive** she would be successful in all she did. This was a complete turnaround for her. You've probably seen her. She's a famous super model. She's rich. Her favorite pastime is shopping.

What you put your attention on will increase or decrease. If you place your attention on how bad the world is, then your world will be bad. If you place your attention on how good the world is, then your world will be good. Specifically, what are you placing your attention on?

Looking back over the last few days and weeks I have specifically placed my attention on _____

_____

and _____

_____

ATTENTION IS INTENT

Our big book of word origins links the word 'intent' as coming from 'tendere' which means to stretch. From *'tendere'* (*intendere*) comes the word attention. When you intend, you place your attention inward. That is, you stretch yourself inward with your attention. The word *'intendere'* is to stretch inward, to be directed at, to have purpose, or to plan. The ability to do this, to place your attention inward, is your **power**.

Intent is the power which moves yesterday to tomorrow.

You will do what you intend to do when you put your attention on what
you intend.

_____

_____

_____

_____

Fill in the following: I _____ intend to finish this workbook.

We hope you have written the correct word. However, no matter what you *do*, you will always be correct. You can't make a mistake in this book. After all, you are simply getting to know yourself. In fact, isn't this what life is all about?

INTENT

Intent is a subtle force which glues together the moments of now. It is very powerful because it accesses the source of your being. What you are and what you have . . . that is, "how you have helped yourself," has developed moment to moment in overlaid patterns of <u>now</u> as directed by intent from the source of your being, your essence.

Essence may be understood when it is contrasted to personality. A metaphor is a term which comes from Latin. 'Meta' is beyond, and 'phora' is to carry or transfer. So metaphor means to carry you beyond normal thinking. A good metaphor for essence is the seed of a peach. The outer meat would be like your personality. For your essence to grow, your seed must germinate in the fertile ground of your personality.

Naturally, after a peach drops from the tree, the seed is nourished by the thick outer covering of the fruit. The seed sprouts in an environment provided by its own meat. **The deepest purpose of your intent is to start the process by which your essence, your seed, begins to grow on its own.** Your

You are not your body. You are not your emotions. You are not your mind.

Your essence is beyond description.

_____

_____

_____

_____

personality, 'you,' provides the nourishment to allow essence to grow. The mystics say **'You' must die before you die.** This means the external personality must give energy for the inner essence to live.

GO DEEPER

You can use metaphor to help you understand yourself. This is important because when you know who you are, you will know what you want. Drawing a metaphor of yourself is making a picture which will carry you beyond normal thinking.

One of our readers, Karen Fitzpatrick, was unsure of the idea of drawing a metaphor of her essence. We asked her to clear her mind and relax, and let an image arise. She said she was standing in a tunnel full of white light. In front of her an object glowed, and it wanted her to follow it. As she followed, we asked if she could move into the object, to become the object. When she became the glowing object, the tunnel opened and she beheld a beautiful vista. She realized the vista was her potential, the essence that had always existed within.

It is important to remember that whatever images you select as your metaphor are really a part of you. If you can enter and expand the metaphorical parts of your self you will see what you intend to do with yourself and where your passion lies.

Now **intend** to make a visual description, a metaphor, of your essence. Start by relaxing and allowing an image to come in your mind. Now, go deeper. What is inside that image? When you have finished, write down in

You create your reality. You can bring Heaven to the Earth.

How does creativity work? How do you create?
. . . you make it up.
How would you create Heaven on Earth?

_____

_____

_____

_____

detail the sights and sounds you experienced.

Note: If you are stuck here, perhaps you should order **MANUAL TO BRING HEAVEN TO EARTH**© by **WISDOMGAME®.** This is a thirty day, 180 page program to bring heaven to (your) Earth and develop human creative potential. How does creativity work? It's simple. If you don't know the answer, you **make it up!** If you're stuck whenever we ask you to write something, all you have to do is make it up. Just **make it up.**

Now, place your attention inward, and **intend** to make a visual description of your essence.

My essence looks like _____

_____

_____

_____

_____

_____.

<u>BREAK TIME</u>

Stand up. Throw this book down and exclaim:

At last I'm free to be me!

Of course you are, who else could you be? To show you what depth this

You're free. You've always been free. You will always be free.

Give yourself permission to be whoever you want to be.

_____

_____

_____

_____

question holds, we want you to try another exercise. This will work especially well if you are in a public place. Again, stand up. This time wave your arms as if calling out to someone. Call loudly, as if they were walking away and you wanted their attention. Call so everyone around you can hear you. The person you are calling is you.

Call: **Hey! (your name), come back!**

No one is going to answer, and chances are no one is even going to notice because who cares anyway, and who knows your name in a crowd of people you don't know. So now, no fear! Call again:

Call: **Hey! (your name), come back!**

You will learn a lot about yourself by doing, or not doing this exercise. If you didn't do it, you really should do it sometime. The effect on your spirit is exhilarating. You'll understand just how important you are, and you may understand that you are not your name. Your essence is much deeper than the outside shell of your personality. After doing this exercise you may even feel that your spirit has returned, or that a certain resistance or barrier has been overcome.

You have the right not to be negative.

Change of being is impossible unless you change. Change negatives to
positives. Your being attracts your life.

_____

_____

_____

_____

I did this exercise. Yes, or no: _____.

In doing this exercise I experienced _____

_____

_____

_____.

I thought it was _____

_____.

RESISTANCE

Often, in our lives, we can see where we want to be, but the distance from where we are now to there just seems too great. We become frustrated. The life now we are living is not the now we intend to live. It is as if we are standing on a cliff. We can see the other side, yet directly in front of us is a deep canyon, one which seems impossible to cross. Use your creativity to **make up** a solution right now. How do you get across a deep canyon?

All you do is _____

_____

_____.

Or more simply, _____

_____.

The bridge from here to a fantastic future is built on increasing the brilliance of the pictures in your mind.

As you concentrate and picture it, a brighter future is drawn to you.
This is the law.

_____

_____

_____

_____

PAY ATTENTION

What you pay attention to increases. If you believe that the chasm is too wide, it will get wider. If you believe you can get to the other side, then you will. Sometimes you can climb down the wall and back up the other side, but that wastes a lot of time. You need to build a bridge from here to the other side. This is a bridge to your new reality, where you really and truly have what you want. What does that bridge look like? Is it a wooden bridge? A brick bridge? A suspension bridge? What color is it? Does it make a noise? Is there a toll? Describe it here:

_____

_____

_____

_____

_____.

Now, see if you can't actually draw a picture of it in the space below.

Draw a picture here of the bridge to your new self.

THERE IS A TOLL

There is a cost to get across. However, the price you have to pay to get to the other side is quite small from the viewpoint of where you are going. Here,

The one constant of life is change.

Every eleven months all the cells of your body create an entirely new body. See yourself as young, healthy, and renewed and you will create that in your life.

_____

_____

_____

_____

now, it may seem large.

Once, there was a hundred-year-old man, who had never been sick. One day he had a small sniffle so he went to the doctor. "You're in amazing shape for a hundred year old man," the doctor said. "Really," replied the old man. "If I knew I was going to live this long, I would of taken better care of myself."

When you cross the great river, you will look back at the raft that has brought you across and think, "Why didn't I just come across in a yacht?" While the chasm you need to cross to have everything you want may seem impossibly wide, you have actually created it in your thoughts. The bridge to cross it is also in your thoughts. There is a toll you have to pay.

The truth is, if you are looking to change you have to pay a price. You **actually have to change**. Yes, it's true. To get to the other side you can't stay the same. You actually have to change, but change is good. When you reach the other side of the chasm, the other shore, where you want to be, where you have **Helped Yourself** to what the world has to offer, then you will be a fuller, bigger, newer person. Then your old self will appear as a dim representation of the superior person you have become. You will say "Why didn't I just use my jet and fly across?"

Pundits say "You can't teach an old dog new tricks." But you're not a dog. You're a human being that wants to strip themselves of the chains that bind them to a life of lack. You want more. You want money, love, and more life, more fun. You deserve it. What's holding you back?

Chains of fear and violence, father to son and mother to daughter, bind families, societies, and nations.

You can break the chain when you stand and proclaim "YES!" to what you want.

_____

_____

_____

_____

THE CHAINS OF FEAR

The chains of fear connect from generation to generation, and whole societies are locked in their own self-created double binds. Worry and fear are the anticipation that the future will be unpleasant. The mind becomes so wrapped up in projecting unpleasant outcomes that we can't appreciate or enjoy the moment of now. We want to change but fear it, imagining that when it arrives life will be worse than it is now. This immobilizes us. The fearful person is bound, unable to move to a better life.

The truth sets us free. When the truth about fear is understood, fear is simply dropped. What are you afraid of? Can you write it down, or are you afraid someone will read this? Or, are you afraid of facing your fears? Are you in a double bind of fearing to find out that you have fears? Write it down:

I fear _____

_____

_____

_____.

And also _____

_____

_____

_____.

Now, if you skip the writing above, what are you afraid of? Everyone has

Fear is the construct of an unenlightened mind.

> **If you fear doing something, experience the feelings**
> **. . . then do it anyway.**

_____

_____

_____

_____

fears. Do you fear the opposite sex? Fear going to the dentist or doctor? Are you afraid of going fast? Afraid of getting cancer? Are you afraid of your parents, sister, brother? Of getting old? Are you afraid of someone finding out who you really are inside? Afraid of change? Success? Afraid of rejection? Afraid of death?

Write more:

I fear _____

_____

_____

_____

_____ .

You would be a very unusual person if you weren't afraid of something or someone. But since you're reading this, we know you are unusual. **You're special.** You are unique. When you understand why fear appears, and when you understand what fear is, then without drama, simply and easily you drop fear. What would life be like without fear? If a movie were made about your life without fear, what would that look like?

I see a movie of my life. I am fearless in that movie. Right away I _____

_____ ,

And_____

Seeing is doing.

When you look you'll see that most people are sleeping through their lives. They experience reality through a lens of judgment. As you begin seeing this you will stop comparing yourself to others and be able to do. You're waking up.

_____

_____

_____

_____

FEAR

It almost makes you shudder just to hear the word. But "almost" only scores points in horse shoes. Right now, we are going to eradicate fear, and we're not afraid to do it!

If you walk in the hills on a path and you see a snake, what happens? Most people get out of the way quick. Snakes can bite you and kill you, so this is a spontaneous and natural reaction. There is no time involved. There is no separation between your awareness of the danger and the reaction to the danger. As you see you do. **Seeing is doing.**

It's good to be prepared. When you started the hike you may have had concerns that you would run into a snake, so you took a snake bite kit. Once prepared, you dropped anxiety. Worry and fear arise because we believe that the future holds danger for which you couldn't possibly be prepared. Worry and fear appear because we remove ourselves from the ever present now.

The truth will set you free, and the truth is that **the only time that exists is now.** If you believe that the future is like a mine field and to help yourself you've got to walk through that mine field, then you probably won't even take the first step. The world's not a mine field. It's a feast and it's free for the asking. The first step is to see your fears and drop your fears.

The Law of Attraction says: That which is like unto itself is drawn.

The pictures that you see and hold and attach emotions to are magnetically drawn to you.

_____

_____

_____

_____

SEEING IS DOING

Being afraid takes you away from seeing. It blinds you and immobilizes you so you can't participate and enjoy the feast. Hidden deep within fear is tremendous energy. You can access this energy when you look at your fear. If you can feel your fear and take action, the bound energy will be released. Your frozen being will be transformed into positive action.

Be your fear and look at the world. It has changed. Doors are opening. People and places are calling. Anticipate good and the good is drawn to you. You are a great person. You will succeed at whatever you do.

You are wonderful!

RE-READ THIS BOOK

Now, go back and re-read this book and look at what you have written. Notice how you feel and notice the changes. Soon, everything you have desired will come to you because you have **Helped Yourself.**

You are a wonderful person!

CHAPTER 3

<u>THINK</u> **<u>BIG</u>**

Once there was a traveler quite like all of us, intelligent, good looking and very friendly, and also quite curious. This person made a long journey that was filled with difficult trials. They climbed over mountains of travail and through valleys filled with sloughs of despond. They traversed rivers of sorrow and hacked through jungles of mud to try and understand themselves. Finally they heard about a mysterious king called Wazawaza who was especially known for his ability to adapt his wisdom to any situation.

The traveler was a curious soul and sent out letter after letter and made unending phone calls overseas to find Wazawaza and make an appointment. Finally, almost by accident, an appointment was arranged and the weary traveler crossed several continents, took planes, and trains, and buses and finally an old oxen pulled them through the jungle to the hut of King Wazawaza, but still the King's councils would not allow an audience. Weeks passed, and then at last a break through.

"Send them in!" barked King Wazawaza.

Indignantly, the curious seeker bowed before King Wazawaza. "Your highness I have a small favor to ask of you."

"Throw em out," yelled Wazawaza, "until dey they learn dat you insult me by asking for anything small."

The essence of whatever you give your attention to is unfolding in your experience.

There is nothing you cannot be, have, or do.

_____

_____

_____

_____

Think **BIGGER**

What if everything changed to be much, much better? Not just that you got what you want but that you got so much more that everything changed. All the stuff that's bothering you now just disappeared. What would that be like? Write it down.

Everything changed. My world is now _____

_____

_____

_____

_____.

I feel _____

_____.

I have

1._____

2._____

3_____

4._____

5._____.

I am

_____

_____.

The longer you can hold an exact picture in your mind without change, the more rapidly it will manifest.

Wishes are desires: desires become thoughts; thoughts form ideas. Ideas rule the world.

_____

_____

_____

_____

I also have_____

_____.

THE WISHING TREE

Once there were twin brothers who weren't exactly alike. One had such a pleasing personality that everybody fell for him. The other could solve any problem. Although their family was very rich, when they grew into manhood they donned old rags and set out on an adventure. As they traveled, they met up with a caravan and were introduced to the King and Queen. Immediately their daughter, a beautiful princess, fell madly in love with the charming brother, but the King would not have it.

"Take them to the edge of the world and throw them off!"

The queen knew better. She whispered to her personal guard. "Knock them out. Take the charming one to the castle dungeon and give me the key. I'll teach him some real manners. Take the other one to the edge of the world and throw him away."

When the problem-solving brother woke up at the edge of the world his life had been spared, but he was confused and could only follow along with a group of people who found their way to a cage where there was a talking lion.

"Where's my brother?" asked the twin.

"How should I know?" replied the lion.

119

The stories we tell ourselves make the moving pictures that run through our minds.

Change the stories about your past and you change what will occur in your future.

_____

_____

_____

_____

"I wish to find my brother."

"Free me," whispered the lion, "and I will take you to the wishing tree."

That night the twin released the lion, and the beast led him through the forest where they found the wishing tree.

"My wish," said the brother, "Is to be reunited with my twin."

The sky opened and the dark night sky flashed. Immediately, the two twins were back together. Unfortunately, they were locked in the dark in the dungeon.

GO BACK

Take a little time right now and go back and read what you have written earlier as your wishes. Turn back now. Write down the two most important wishes.

1._____

_____.

2._____

_____.

For every cause there is an effect.

Ask yourself this: Am I causing my life to move as I want it to happen, or am I being moved by forces beyond my comprehension and control?

_____

_____

_____

_____

KARMA

Karma is an easy concept to understand, but first consider this phrase: "Be careful what you wish, you might get it." What do you think of that?

It's_____.

Perhaps you wrote "It's rubbish." Or maybe you wrote, "That could be true." If you didn't write anything, then go back and write "What goes around is what comes around." This is a very close approximation of what Karma means.

Karma is a Sanskrit word meaning "comeback." The Earth circles the Sun. The Moon circles the Earth. The weather goes through the cycles of spring, summer, fall, winter, and then comes back to spring. Occurrences in our lives tend to recur. Friends seem to cycle back again and again. We tend to live and relive the same days, and our actions seem to reap the same rewards over and over.

COME BACK

But as it turned out, since the one twin brother could solve any problem, he was able to pick the lock, and soon they escaped. As they made their way out of the dungeon, a beautiful young girl called out from a cell, "Please help me!" The problem-solving twin easily unlocked the massive door.

"My mother, the evil Queen, has imprisoned me."

"You're free," said the problem-solving brother. Come with us."

The Principle of Correspondence says, "As above, so below."

Nature hides a great paradox. While we can approach reality we can never know it exactly. . . But you don't have to know "exactly" how something works to use it. Emotions added to images create reality.

_____

_____

_____

_____

"You're so handsome," said the girl.

Stepping forward the charming twin brother bowed. "Thank you."

"No, I mean you, the one who opened the door." replied the young princess.

You see, the evil Queen had imprisoned one of her own daughters. Together, the brothers and the young princess escaped, searched out and found her sister, the other young princess, and they all returned to the brother's homeland and lived happily ever after.

So, you never know.

LIFE IS RELATIVE

It happened during the Civil War. A man and his two young sons were very prosperous farming tobacco. One day the two sons were racing their horses. They collided and the first son broke his leg, and the second son broke both his arms. The neighbors lamented. "You'll never bring in a crop now. Your farm is ruined. What a terrible tragedy." All the farmer could reply was "Maybe."

That week the Southern army rode into town and conscripted all the young men for soldiers, but the farmer's sons were spared because of their broken bones. When the neighbors got together with the farmer they cried, "How lucky you are. You're family has been spared." All the farmer could say was "Maybe."

The very next week as the farmer and his wife slept, the first son hobbled to the stove to make breakfast and as he lit the stove, he spilled the grease. The

The ideal state is freedom of movement.

> **The blocks which prevent your freedom are barriers you have constructed from an earlier time. They are mental constructs which can easily be replaced by images of freedom which deconstruct those blocks.**

What do you think?

_____

_____

_____

_____

fire spread and all the two sons could do was to wake up the farmer and his wife and get out of the house before it burned to the ground. The tobacco caught fire and the farm was ruined.

The neighbors tried to help, but it was too late. "What misery! What a disaster!" They screamed. "Well. . . " said the farmer as the family gathered their belongings. "Maybe."

From the distant hills the commanders of the Northern army sighted the fire. "We've taken that town. Move the troopes South." The war passed by the farmer's town. The farmer rebuilt and was very successful.

So, you never know.

BARRIERS

Some people say "It's my karma," when what they mean is "I'm stuck and there's nothing I can do about it." As was pointed out before, what you pay attention to will increase. Do you believe that an action in a past life or that some action in this life is stopping you from helping yourself right now? Are you concentrating your attention on the problem instead of the solution?

There will always be barriers to you having what you want. Some will be easy to overcome, and some will be difficult. A barrier to one person may appear large, but to others it may be small.

Rex Talmage tells this story:

"I was vacationing in a small town on the coast of California. Even though it was the middle of winter, the day was very nice. While the rest of the

Anything is possible.

If you can think of it, you can do it.

_____

_____

_____

_____

country was snowed in, the sun heated the beach and the afternoon sand was warm. Walking along the edge of the water, with my mind lost in reverie, I didn't notice a small river in front of me. It was about six feet across, looked about a foot deep, and ran out to large waves in the ocean.

"I thought, my walk is over. I'll have to turn around. There was no way to get across.

"While I stood there contemplating this small twist of fate, some young children ran playfully next to me. They paused for an instant, then they took off their shoes and carried them across as they ran through the little river to the other side.

"I could see it was only my belief that kept me back, so I took off my shoes and waded through and continued my beach walk."

YOU'RE SPECIAL

You are a very special person. You are a valuable, unique, one of a kind being. No one is exactly like you. Congratulations! Bravo! You are wonderful. Yes, you are special.

However, your problems and whatever barriers you experience are not unique. Throughout time and right now, many other people have experienced, and are experiencing, the same barriers. Some move across quickly. Others

We live and move in the realm of energy.

Our well-being and our ability to accomplish depends on the amount of energy we are capable of wielding.

_____

_____

_____

_____

need a device to get across. A device that has helped others see their barriers is "**If only**." Please fill in the following.

If only I had _____

_____.

If only_____

_____.

If only_____

_____.

Barriers can be big or small. If you haven't or you can't fill in all of the above 'If onlys' maybe you are afraid of actually overcoming your barriers. Or, now you're bored, or you don't think it's important. Perhaps you think this whole book is ridiculous (That's okay. Laughter is the best medicine.) Maybe you can't access any "if onlys." Write again.

If only _____

_____.

If only _____

_____.

How do you get through barriers? You can place some dynamite and blast through. You can dig underneath, undermine the supports, and let the barriers

Professional athletes train and train toward perfection.

To manifest your desires you must train your mind to hold images that
are infused with positive emotions. This ability exists within and is
already perfect. You can use it to get what you want.

_____

_____

_____

_____

fall by themselves. You can tie them to balloons so they float away. You can melt them with heat vision. You can take them out in the trash. You can erase them.

Right now, understand the **barrier actually is** the **"if only."** More exactly, *it is your belief* in underlying lack that doesn't allow you to have what the "if only" represents. Agree? For instance, perhaps you said, "*If only* I had a million dollars, my problems would be over." It's your belief you don't have and can't have a million dollars which creates the "if only." This is your barrier to having a million dollars.

You do have a million dollars! **The world is a feast.** It's simply your belief that you can't have a million dollars which creates the barrier. Without 'if only' you would already be doing what needs to be done. .

Go back to every "If only . . ." which you have filled in on the previous pages and write over them in big bold letters: **Don't Exist!** You can have whatever you want. You can help yourself because the world is a feast.

PARASITIC ACTION

A parasite is something that steals energy from its host. When we begin to help ourselves, we may be making actions which drain our energies. These "parasitic" actions keep us from getting what we want. That is, getting what we want would be easy and simple if we didn't work against ourselves.

When a professional athlete catches a pass or does a triple spin on ice or streaks across the finish line, they appear to be poetry in motion. They do

Banish worry.

Worry is looking back at pictures of the past and projecting negative outcomes on the future. It creates a negative future. Replace worry with pictures of happy outcomes and have faith.

_____

_____

_____

_____

what they do with a total absence of resistance because they have trained their bodies to perform flawless movement. They have removed any actions that are unnecessary or extraneous. To move smoothly and flawlessly through life we must also remove parasitic actions.

We need to be like golfers who videotape their swings so they can see the errors and correct their movements. If we want to move through life as poetry in motion like professional athletes, we need to find the distracting forces in our beings which act as parasites and steal our energy. We find these in a hidden place called the shadow.

THE SHADOW

There is nothing to fear. Fear is a mental construct of an unenlightened mind which we create to take us away from facing the ever present now. The shadow is not fearful. It is simply a place in our consciousness that we are unaware of.

Here is a simple exercise to bring you to the moment of now:

Stamp your feet on the ground and say, "This is the ground." If you're outside touch a tree or bush and say, "This is a tree. This is a bush."

Look up. Say "That is the sky." Touch your body. "This is me." If you are inside, touch the wall. Say "This is the wall." Point up. "That is the ceiling." Touch your desk. "This is my desk." Now, wherever you are, touch your arm and say, "This is my arm." Now touch your chest. "This is my chest."

The world is alive.

The rocks, the plants, the trees, the animals and the air itself are vibrating at different rates. Everything is in a constant state of flux and change is the only constant.

_____

_____

_____

_____

Say "I'm here. The time is now." Touch your surroundings, say "This is the wall, that's the window." Point at the ceiling. "That is the ceiling." Stomp on the floor. "This is the floor." Continue doing this until you feel the feeling: **I'm here. The time is now.**

Jonathan didn't know why he couldn't get a date. As a handsome young assistant professor at the university with a new car and a nice apartment, he looked good on paper. He wasn't bad looking either. Whenever he met a nice girl, he stepped up to the plate, took a few good swings, but he always struck out. He couldn't see in his shadow why he wasn't in a relationship. Tired, lonely, and frustrated at last he discovered **WISDOMGAME®.** He ordered **The Art of Fascinating the Opposite Sex©** and his life changed.

Jonathan discovered himself in his relationship to others. Hidden in his shadow was the belief that he had to be better than the women he wanted to date. As he learned the art of fascinating, he found out that when he approached women he had an artificial smile. Actually, he wasn't very happy and came across as aloof and condescending. Because he pretended to himself that he was perfect, he projected that women had to be perfect too. Since no one is perfect, no one could fit the perfect slipper he was offering. As he shone the light of consciousness into his shadow, he discovered his reality and he helped himself. You can too.

You can **Help Yourself. The world is a feast. Everything is here just for the asking. All you have to do is ask.**

As you become filled with light, your power to affect the world around you increases.

> You become a radiating beacon of energy which gathers strength and reaches higher.

_____

_____

_____

_____

CONSCIOUS LIGHT

You are walking down a dark hallway. There is rug on the floor and you feel the walls as you inch ahead toward a dim light. Now, this long hallway is getting a little lighter. It's not so dim, and you can just make out ahead of you light coming from a skylight in the ceiling. Finally, you are right under the skylight and as you look up you see the sky. You see the sun is behind dark clouds. As you look at the dark clouds, instantly they part and the sun shines into your eyes.

This light is created by your mind and can't hurt your mental eyes so now you absorb as much of your own light as you desire. When you shine the light of your mind into the shadows of your consciousness, you wake up to what you have been hiding from yourself. When "parasitic" actions, which you created for whatever reasons, become obvious then you easily drop them and **help yourself.**

Once there was a person who was wrongly accused, tried, convicted, and sentenced to be held in a dark prison. Days, weeks, months and years went by and they existed, always in the dark. Then one day their rusted chains broke and though weak and feeble they crawled out of their cell. They crawled through the hallways and corridors, and at last the doorway to the outside opened. Intense bright light filled the opening, but there in the light a figure stood so filled with light it could hardly be seen. It spoke.

"At last!" cried the figure. "At last some shade! This intense light has been killing me."

At the point of now, there are choices.

Your choices make you who you are.

_____

_____

_____

_____

IT'S YOUR CHOICE

You can get caught up in wanting, or you can have so much you want to chuck it all and return to another time in your life when things seemed simple. You are a powerful person. The choices that you make are important for your life and for everyone else too. The giant, macro world of society, politics, and international relations is an extension of the smaller, micro world of your life. What you think and what you do matters to everyone in the world. There is no such thing as one person's little world. You world is not "little." **What you do matters**.

You are a cause in the fabric of reality that greatly matters to everyone else in the world. The actions that you take have a wave-like ripple effect. How you are, how you do, creates your world and your world influences the whole world. Feel good about yourself. Know that by helping yourself to the world's feast you are helping others to help themselves.

YOU CAN HELP YOURSELF.

You are unlimited!

You are a terrific person!

CHAPTER 4

<u>A THOUSAND WORDS</u>

In this workbook one thousand words is approximately four pages of text. If you will write four pages about each item you want to manifest in your life they will manifest. For instance, if you could describe in detail the new home you would like to live in, or the new job you would like to have, or your new lover, or whatever you desire then those wishes would be attracted to you much more quickly. But four pages is a lot of writing, and some people would find it difficult. There's an easier way.

A picture is worth a thousand words. For the next section of **The World's a Feast**© you will need scissors and glue or some clear plastic tape. Remember, this workbook is a record of your wants, wishes and desires. It is designed so that you can review it over and over. If you use it, it will quickly produce in reality whatever you want. But for those things to manifest in your life you have to take a little time right now and fill in the blanks. If you have been reading through this workbook, congratulations! Now you are very educated. If you have been filling in the blanks, getting to know yourself, that is fantastic! You are manifesting what you want. Soon, you're life will change. This change will be accelerated if you do the following:

In the beginning of this workbook, on page 39, you wrote down five wishes. Go back now and review them. If you didn't put anything down, or if your wishes have changed, rewrite them. List your five wishes here:

Wishing is perfecting desire.

Recognize that what you have now is what you previously wanted and that anything that is less than perfect is illusion. Your wishes come true.

_____

_____

_____

_____

FIVE WISHES

My five wishes:

1. _____

   _____.

2. _____

   _____.

3. _____

   _____.

4. _____

   _____.

5. _____

   _____.

(Remember: If you can't think of a wish to write, **make up something!**)

You may have wished for a new house, or a lover, or a better job, or money, or a wife or husband, or another car, or kids, or a vacation, or a new pet. Whatever your wish, you can find a picture that represents it.

What you consistently picture comes true.

Beliefs create reality.

Allow yourself to have more than you have ever dreamed possible.

_____

_____

_____

_____

Bill and Betty Smart tell this story:

"When we were first married we lived in a little cramped apartment. We both had jobs and were doing pretty well. When Betty got pregnant we had to find a larger place so we took a drive out of state. Just for a lark we took pictures of some of the homes in a fine neighborhood. Back at the apartment, when we looked at the pictures, one property really appealed to us. Every night we looked at it, thought about what a nice place it would be for our children. For fun we stuck it in an envelop and mailed it to ourselves.

"Last year, after Bill got his promotion we actually moved. When we unpacked our things, an unopened letter fell out of the boxes. We both smiled when we opened it. It was the picture of the house we had taken a while back. Amazingly, it was a picture of a house exactly like the one we moved into."

Picture Smart

Where do you get a picture of your wish? You can do as the Smarts did, and take a picture of what you want, or you can print it off the Internet. You can buy a magazine, or you can go to the library and use the duplicator and copy a picture. For instance, if you wished for a certain type of dog, you might see the exact type in a dog magazine. Get that magazine, cut out the picture of the dog, and paste it in the space provided below. This is a fun project. Have fun doing it. Don't put any limits on what you want. Cut out pictures of what you would really like to have regardless of the monetary value.

You have abundance in every area of your life.

Expect it to happen and it will.

_____

_____

_____

_____

If your wish is to have more money, what you are going to do is to take your bank statement, white out the amount in your balance and write in or type in the new amount you desire. Then make a copy of that statement and glue or paste it in the space for one of your wishes. Or, you could make out a personal check paid to yourself for a million dollars or whatever amount you desire, and then paste it in the space for a wish. If you don't have a bank account, or a checkbook, you can find a picture of gold coins, or gold blocks, or a picture of dollars. And finally, if you can't find any of those, then take a coin out of your pocket and use a pencil and draw around it. This is your lucky multiplier coin. Every time you see this picture, this coin will double in worth.

A $1000 WORD

This is a very, very important section. A picture is worth much more than a thousand words. In fact, it could be worth more than a million dollars a word. You are on the beginning of an adventure which leads you to the pot of gold at the end of the rainbow. You have captured the leprechaun, and he's about to reward you five wishes. For every picture you find and enter in the spaces below, the magic lantern is being rubbed and the wish-granting Genie bows before your desires.

Every time you look at these pictures, and whenever you review this workbook, these pictures will be etched in your subconscious mind and sooner than you think these pictures will become your reality. Have fun taking or finding these pictures and cutting them out and have fun putting

149

If you want something from somebody, then make a picture of a time in which you gave that same thing to someone else.

Hold positive pictures and you attract positive outcomes.

_____

_____

_____

Note: Remember that the lines and spaces above are for your comments.

them in their spaces. Get used to enjoying life and having fun, because very soon whatever you desire will be manifest. The purpose of **WISDOMGAME®** is to educate, entertain, and enlighten. You deserve it. You are a wonderful person. You can **Help Yourself. Find five pictures of your wishes and tape or paste them in the spaces below.**

FIRST WISH

Realize your passion by picturing your path.

Use your imagination to picture the highest path you can take.

_____

_____

_____

_____

SECOND WISH

Use your imagination.

> Let your imagination create pictures, and then create a vision of the life you'd love to live.

_____

_____

_____

_____

THIRD WISH

Imagine having all the money, love, friendship, and objects that you want.

Hold on to feelings that come with these imaginations and amplify them.

_____

_____

_____

_____

FOURTH WISH

No limits!

Create pictures that glow. Create images that vibrate with all the feelings
you have within you. Reach for the stars.
You will succeed!

_____

_____

_____

_____

FIFTH WISH

Wisdom is gained through experience.

When you create an image in your mind and demonstrate it in your world, you will gain from the experience and be able to demonstrate more and more of whatever your want.

_____

_____

_____

_____

WISDOMGAME®

Wisdom is knowledge gained through experience.

It's true: one great book recently published was *What We Actually Know About the Human Mind.* Somehow it got through the editor, and the publisher. Maybe it was the fault of the printer, but when the book came out all the pages were blank. It became the rage. Everyone wanted to know what we really know about ourselves, but what we know is nothing compared to what we don't know. We're always learning and growing. We're a work in progress. The book, and the revelation of blank pages, was a great experience for many people. When they opened the book and saw the blank pages they understood their lives can be whatever they make of them. The book sold over ten million copies.

Wisdomgame® is experiential. This means we believe that to live life, you must have experiences. Since seeing is doing, by creating the picture book above, you are experientially creating true wishes. Right now, you are going to take another real action.

Find the scissors and the glue or tape you used with the pictures above. At the top of the next page is a dotted line. Turn to the next page and look at it. Cut out the page, fold it up, put on a stamp and send it to us.

This *is* a test.

Take action now.

Join Wisdomgame

Join our world-wide network of artists, writers, photographers, inventors and creative people.

Wisdomgame.org

_____

_____

_____

_____

This action tests your intent. It is a simple test to see if you are willing

to take action, to spend the tiny cost of a stamp and the energy of putting

it in the mailbox . . . to actually do something to get what you want in life.

TAKE ACTION NOW! Wisdom is created through experience. By

sending out this mailer **you are doing.** You have **Helped Yourself. Cut this**

page out of the workbook now and mail it in.

MAGIC BOX- 1 _____ CUT HERE _____

(duplicate this page and send it to us.)

_____ **FOLD-BACK HERE** _____ ____

FROM _____   STAMP   ☐ HERE
      _____
      _____

                    TO: **Wisdomgame.org**
                        17230 Rayen St.
                        Northridge,
                        California   91325

___ _____

                    Fold back on line

Put wish here: _____

                    _____

              tape together here

163

Is destruction part of creativity?

Remove this page and mail it to:

Wisdomgame
17230 Rayen St.
Northridge, Ca 91325

You are much larger than you know.

Good. If you followed the instructions above, you cut out the page, wrote in your wish, put on a stamp and sent the wish to us. Nothing can stop this wish from coming true. Soon, very soon, you will have helped yourself to whatever you desire.

The letter above is your first magic box. By cutting it out of this workbook and sending it to **Wisdomgame®,** you have taken a real step toward actualizing your dreams. The magic box above is linked to a second magic box below.

MAGIC BOX - 2

Lines left empty for later.

1._____

2._____

3._____

4._____

You are much larger than you know.

YOU ARE UNLIMITED!

CHAPTER 5

BE POLITE

Don Bernstien was raised in the Jewish tradition of storytelling. Some of the little kids were pushing each other and being rude before the dinner, so Don gathered the family together and told this story:

"Once upon a time a young girl married a man a little older then her. She really loved him and wanted to have a family with him, but the thing was he was mean. She didn't want her kids to turn out mean and rude like him so she waited a while to get pregnant. But then as time went by she did.

"Pretty soon she started showing and as her belly grew she came up with the idea to gently pat her stomach and say, 'Be polite. Be polite.' At three months everyone could see she was going to have kids. She patted her stomach and said, 'Be polite. Be polite.'

"At four, five, and six months she kept patting her stomach gently and saying, 'Be polite. Be polite.' Seven, and eight months she said, 'Be polite. Be polite.' When nine months came around she was pretty large but no babies came out.

"At ten and eleven months, still no babies but she kept patting her stomach and saying 'Be polite, be polite.' Five years, no babies. Ten years, no

We shape ourselves by the stories we tell ourselves.

_____

_____

_____

_____

babies. Fifty years went by and the lady died. 'Quick!' the neighbors shouted, 'Get those babies out!'

"When they pulled out the babies they were old men with grey beards. As they came out the first one stopped and looked at the second one. 'After you,' he said., 'No, no,' replied the second, 'After you.' 'No,' said the first, 'I insist. After you '

"No. No. After you."

"No. No. After you."

Too Polite

Are you being too polite with yourself? Are you waiting for one part of you to come forward while another part of you waits on you to step out? Are you a schlemiel (chump) or a schlimazel (habitual failure)?

It's true, at that very dinner, in front of the whole family, Don Bernstien asked this question: "How can you tell the difference between a schlemiel and a schlimazel?" One of the teenagers jumped up.

"I know," he said. "A schlemiel always butters his toast on both sides. . ."

Then his brother jumped up and interrupted. "But a schlimazel's toast always falls butter side down."

"You're both right," Don laughed. "When the Schlemiel brings in the soup for mama, he trips, and the soup spills all over the Schlimazel."

Illusions

Illusions continue to exist because people give them energy by putting attention on them. When energy is taken away from the illusion it disintegrates.

_____

_____

_____

_____

You're Wonderful

You're not a schlimazel or schlemiel. You are a successfully fantastic person who holds the key to unlocking the abundance of the world. You can have all the love, friendship, money, and material processions which you desire. . . . But you may be too polite with yourself. You have great work to do. Remember:

Grab the ass of life and drag it to you.

WHAT ARE YOU WAITING FOR?

As soon as

_____

_____,

then I am going to help myself to the feast of the world.

As soon as

_____

_____,

then I am going to help myself to the life I want.

You have the right to remain silent.

If you find yourself in a negative mood and want to complain . . . Stop! You have the right to remain silent.

_____

_____

_____

_____

172

As soon as

_____

_____ ,

then I am going to help myself to all the love I want.

STOP!

Go back to the three "As soon as" statements you wrote. Cross them out and write in big letters **NOW I MANIFEST WHAT I WANT!**

By using this workbook you are learning to **Help Yourself.** You are a work in progress. You have taken the first step on your journey. You are on the path to a new, abundant, vibrant life. . . a life full of fun and full of joy.

THE MAGNUM OPUS

In the Latin language the word *Magnum* means great. *Opus* means work. Your great work is your *Magnum Opus*. It is the development of you. It begins in the discovery that you are more than simple flesh and bones, and that you have a mind which can do more than react to circumstances. In fact, your "Great Work," is the discovery that you create yourself AND you create the world.

You have the ability to create a new you and a new world around you to be whatever you wish it to be. Part of the Great Work you are now undertaking is the understanding and use of Universal Forces. When you understand that

You are beautiful, eternal, universal, and infinite.

> The Universal Law, the living Spirit, is unlimited. This Force is within you; therefore you are unlimited.

_____

_____

_____

_____

you and the forces that surround you work together, then getting what you want from life is as easy as snapping your fingers. What you want will appear almost like magic. When you want it, it appears.

UNIVERSAL FORCES

Before the great inventors of the nineteenth century, very little was known about electricity. Before the Second World War in the twentieth century, few people could imagine the use of nuclear power. The use of solar energy and its conversion to electric power is a recent event. Our understanding of our world progresses as we develop.

No one can deny that Universal Forces do exist. Anyone who's been in an earthquake, a snowstorm, or a hurricane, or experienced the devastation of a tornado, or seen a tsunami, or witnessed a volcano exploding knows first-hand the gigantic powers of nature. Anyone who has grown a garden, raised animals, or reared a family knows the subtle strength of nature as it expands and also knows the power of decay and contraction as things get old and die.

The Universe is controlled by the Law of Attraction.

When you understand and live in harmony with the law that states "your being attracts your life," then who you are and how you think produces unlimited abundance.

_____

_____

_____

_____

When we look at the expanse of sky with billions of star systems, or when we contemplate the micro-world of our own atoms, we fall into awe and reverie. Some Force holds everything together. We live our lives surrounded by the people and things we have attracted to us, and in a similar manner our planet, our solar system, and our galaxy live their lives surrounded by things held to them by attraction.

Like Attracts Like

You **Help Yourself** in life by attraction, and the rule is ***like attracts like.*** As Jesus says in the Bible, "To those who have will be given more, and to those who have not it will be taken away." What you focus on increases. If you focus on lack, you attract lack, and lack will increase. If you focus on abundance you attract abundance, and your abundance will increase.

There is kind of a trick you have to play on yourself. If you don't have something, you need to believe that you have it and hold on to that belief as if you had more and more of it. Believe -- really believe -- and those things are yours.

Magnetizing

Bringing the objects, money, and people you want into your life is easy. You do this by putting yourself into a calm state and drawing the images, symbols, and the pictures you desire into your mind. If you have been

Magnetic personal power depends on uniting physical vitality with strong emotional pictures.

By holding vibrant emotional states within your mind those states become charged with energy which can be directed to magnetically attract good to you.

_____

_____

_____

_____

following along in this workbook you already have real pictures pasted them on the page above so you may review them at any time.

Learn to relax, focus, visualize, and use your imagination. As you hold the images of what you desire in your mind's eye, you construct around you a magnetic coil of light. This gigantic magneto pulses with energy which swirls around you. You are the magnetic center of the coil and the energy spirals about you. As this energy speeds around your external body, inside you concentrate on the things you want to attract. Your coil pulses and expands. Light sparkles and jumps from you, goes out into the Universe and pulls objects, money, and people to you. You are now setting the forces of Universal Attraction into play. The more real you make this magneto the more powerful it becomes.

Positive constructive thoughts are highly magnetic. What you love will be attracted to you. Likewise, if you concentrate on something you hate, it will attract hate. You may attract what you desire immediately, or it may take several magnetic visualizations to focus your intent. If the visualization of your coil is strong, and you actually feel the magnetic power within you, your magnetic power will greatly increase.

Personal Magnetism

It is a quite simple matter to develop your personal magnetism so that when you deal with other people they will be greatly influenced. While you are using the magneto visualization exercises to attract those things, money and

Whatever a man sow, that he shall reap.

A smile gets a smile; kind thoughts produce kind thoughts in others. If we live a life of love and kindness, those who we are with will feel the attraction of love and kindness, drawing them to us.

_____

_____

_____

_____

objects you desire, you may also want to increase your personal magnetic power to attract members of your same sex and those of the opposite sex. (Order: **The Art of Fascinating the Opposite Sex©**)

Around every being there is a natural magnetic field called the aura. The word 'aura' is defined as the atmosphere surrounding you. Another word for it is 'nimbus,' which is a circle of radiant light around the head. There are exercises which increase the magnetic attractive power of this circle of light.

As we said in the first part of this manual, for a thing to exist in your world, you need to believe it exists. In your mind's eye, see a circle of white light around your head. Now, expand the circle of light so that it takes the shape of an egg of light around your whole body from your head to you feet. This is your aura.

Lift up your right hand. How did you do that? Did you tell your hand to rise? Did you command it? How did you will that to happen? You learned how to move your arms and your legs when you were a baby, and you put that "how-to" information in your subconscious mind. In a similar way to raising your hand, you can will your aura to be larger, stronger, and more magnetic. The aura becomes more magnetic as you think positive thoughts. You can **Help Yourself** by increasing your personal magnetism. See the circle of light around you increasing and influencing the people around you. As if raising your hand, actually push out the aura to be stronger, vibrant, and more alive.

The word 'enthusiasm' means God within.

_____

_____

_____

_____

Your aura will become very powerful. The more positive and enthusiastic you are about it the stronger and more attractive your aura becomes.

Enthusiasm

To be enthusiastic means to be inspired, to have the strong excitement of feelings, to be passionate with zeal or fervor. The word 'enthusiasm' comes from Greek words *en* which means within and *theos* which means God. To be *enthusiastic* means to be within God, to be like God. How do you do this, especially if you don't feel like it, if you're feeling down?

Wind Horse

The Tibetans have a special name for creating this state of enthusiasm. They call it **'bringing up wind horse.'** When you're depressed, when nothing's going on in your life, when you're bored, or when you're down, it's like the weather pattern before a windstorm.

You can bring up enthusiasm like a wind horse charging through the calm of your life. Instantly you can be feeling alive, passionate, and filled with zeal and fervor. How do you do it?

You do it by being creative. **You create it!** You stir yourself. You pull it up from the interior of you and charge yourself. **You make it up!**

Right now toss this workbook aside. It's not important. You can come back to it later. **<u>You're important!</u>** Your emotional state is important. Feeling good about yourself is the most wonderful thing you can do for yourself. Wrap your hands around your chest and say this ten times:

You are unlimited!

YOU ARE A TERRIFIC PERSON!

I feel terrific!

Now, say it again and again. When you've said it over and over at least ten times then add this to it:

I **DO** feel terrific.!

Again:

I **DO** feel terrific!

Again:

Yes! I do feel terrific!

MAGIC BOX 2

Go back to the blank box marked Magic Box 2 (page 165) and on the first line write this phrase:

My wishes come true.

IT'S FUN!

How you think about life, what you focus on, becomes your reality. The work of helping yourself is easy. It's fun. Once you master the simple

Love, joy, friendship, all the objects, and abundance you desire flow to you easily and without much effort because you support the Universe and the Universe supports you in all that you do.

_____

_____

_____

_____

techniques in the **WISDOMGAME® HOW TO HELP YOURSELF**

SERIES©, your world begins to change. No longer will you be in the dark.

Now you realize you are the light switch; you are the light bulb and in fact

you are the light itself. Turn the pages back to Magic Box 2 (page 165) and

on the second line write this phrase:

Life's fun. I enjoy life.

You're Powerful

Hidden deep within you are currents of strength you may have only

experienced as possibilities . . . but they are real. You are much deeper than

you know, and in fact, you are dynamo of power. As you begin to understand

and experience the unity of your essence as the power of your body coupled

with the strength of your mind . . . nothing . . . **absolutely nothing . . . can**

stop you. On line three of Magic Box 2 (page 165) write this:

I am powerful. The whole world is mine.

The Universe Supports You

When you believe in yourself and begin to actualize your desires, this is the

right way. This supports the order of things. This is the way it was all

intended. The Cosmos, the Universe, and Nature herself is overflowing with

Those things you desire are here now.

Everything that you want-- all your desires-- are manifesting at all times around you because the Universe is abundant and overflowing with good. The World is a feast. It's yours for the asking. Create an image in your mind of what you want and your wishes are granted. This is Universal Law.

_____

_____

_____

_____

abundance. It is your natural right to have whatever you desire. What you desire comes about. Write this on line four of Magic Box 2:

I support the Universe and the Universe support me.

HOW LONG WILL IT TAKE?

It was a beautiful day and a poor man decided to take a walk in the forest. He listened to the sweet sounds of the birds chirping and looked at the flowers blooming in many shapes and colors. The air smelled fresh and clean with the scent of pine. As he walked along the path he noticed the puffy white clouds in the blue sky, and how the spires of the tall trees almost touched the white clouds. Right then next to him, he felt a presence. It was God.

The poor man looked up at the white-haired, beaded figure next to him and with reverence said, "God, may I ask you a question?"

"You just did," replied his Eminence.

"Can I ask you another one?"

"You just did," God replied.

"Seriously," the poor man said as they walked, "What is time?"

God replied, "To me, eternity is like a second."

"What is big?" asked the poor man.

"The Universe is like the head of a pin." replied God.

"What's money?" asked the poor man.

Time is an illusion.

Start now. Visualize what you want. Put positive feelings in that visualization, allow it to happen, and expect it to happen. It will come to you and it will always arrive in the now.

_____

_____

_____

_____

"Trillions and trillions of dollars are like one penny."

The poor man stopped walking. He thought and then turned his face up and looked at God. "God," he said, "can I borrow a penny?"

God laughed to himself and turned back to the poor man and replied. "In a second."

Resolving Time

Why does it take time to attract the objects, money, and people you desire? This is a difficult question to resolve. A paradox is a statement that is seemingly contradictory or opposed to common sense, yet is perhaps true. The paradox is that the time is always now, but it takes time to manifest your dreams.

Now is the only time we exist in. Later today, and tomorrow, and the next day, the time will only be now. When your wishes are granted the time will be now; yet, time has to pass before you reach that now. It seems paradoxical, but it's an artificial barrier. Don't let it bother you. Butterflies don't.

Consider the butterfly. First, it was a worm., then it spent time in a cocoon as a chrysalis, and finally it could fly on the wind. The work you are doing with **WISDOMGAME®** is the forming of your chrysalis. You are spinning a silk web of positive energy around yourself, and sooner than you realize you will be born into a new reality and there take wing, be free, and fly.

The things, the love, the money you desire are on the way to you right now because you desire them. You are a very powerful person. You have the

The Law is simple.

> When you don't believe something is going to happen, it doesn't happen.
> When you believe it will happen, it happens.
> Believe in the Law of Attraction. It works.

_____

_____

_____

_____

ability not only to change yourself in any direction but also to change the world. Your world is not only the surrounding daily life you live. Your world is the continents, the oceans, the nations and people of the world. What you believe and what you believe in matters. **You matter!**

Time is relative to what you believe about time. Your desires can manifest immediately if you believe they can. When you can drop the negative belief that manifestation is impossible, and when you believe in yourself; when you believe that getting what you want is not miraculous but rather the natural outcome of the pictures, words, and thoughts you repeat in your mind; that is, when you rest in faith that what you believe will happen. . . then it happens.

BELIEVE. . . THEN IT HAPPENS.

You are bigger than you think.

You are Unlimited!

CONCLUSION

Take time right now and whenever you feel like it to go back and review what you wrote, drew, and pasted in this workbook. If you haven't cut out the page and sent in your wishes to **WISDOMGAME®** you can go back and do that right now. If you haven't pasted in pictures of your wishes then be on the lookout for magazines you can clip so you can find pictures of the things you desire. In the first of the five spaces below put in today's date. Every time you read through this workbook again add in the next date.

    1. First read-through date   _____.
       (today's date)

    2. Second read-through date _____.

    3. Third read-through date   _____.

    4. Fourth read-through date _____.

    5. Firth read-through date   _____.

Each time you read through this workbook you will gain a perspective on yourself. Right now, you may be saying or thinking that you'll probably not come back and read this again. But you will because you will be helped greatly in your ability to manifest what you desire if you understand the principles involved within these instructions. Read and often re-read this workbook.

Magic

The magicians of olden times were called Mages. They were called this because they knew how to "image." What they saw in their heads came into reality. It's not magic. It's the way the Universe works.

_____

_____

_____

_____

WISDOMGAME®

The World's a Feast! Help Yourself!© is the first level in a ten course system designed to **Entertain, Educate, and Enlighten**, This course is experiential, meaning that Wisdom comes from experiencing. Humans learn by doing. We can study, memorize, and read to our heart's content but until we use our knowledge and learn from our mistakes we won't be wise.

Wisdom comes from doing. There is no other way.

Keep Doing

You are a great work, a **Magnum Opus**. You are a wonderful person. You will receive what you want, and while your desires will change with time, they also will be actualized. Now, because you have started playing **WISDOMGAME®** you are developing into a highly creative person. You will create the life you desire which will be abundant, full of the objects and money you desire, and full of friendship, love, and joy. This is what you have been waiting for, and now it's beginning to happen. . . . but you still need to participate. . . to keep doing. There is no end to personal development.

It's fun! But you need to persevere.

The Chinese Book of Changes, the I Ching, a book designed to read the future, proclaims the light giving, active, strong and spiritual qualities of a

Never, never, never give up.

It is your right to have whatever you want. You can create a new world for yourself and for the people around you. Start now. Be the person you want to be, picture the life you want, and attract it to you.

_____

_____

_____

_____

person's character as being unrestricted by any fixed condition, and therefore conceived of as motion. The I Ching describes this condition by saying

The Creative works sublime success,

Furthering through perseverance.

In the Bhagavad Gita, the great religious book of the East, the religion of Krishna, says

Those who wish for success in works
Sacrifice in the world to the gods
For quickly in the world of men
Success comes born of ritual action

It says: if we wish for success in developing ourselves, in attracting and manifesting objects, relationships, and money, we must give some of our time each day. We must repeat this sacrifice of time over time, through a duration of days. This is ritual action.

Ritual Action

Ritual action can be sacred or profane. That is, each day you can kneel before your particular shrine and reverently attract a better life or you can swear to the heavens and curse about how bad your life is. Either way, whatever action you take on a consistent basis will create, attract and bring that life to you. If you visualize good and continue to affirm that good, your life will be better. If you see only bad luck; if you continue to say nothing

Play the game of life your way. All the answers are within you. Follow your inner wisdom. You are a valuable person. Your path is important. You matter to the world. Accept and love yourself as you are right now and be open to receive.

You will get whatever you desire.

good ever comes to you; if you curse your life as meaningless. . . that is the life you will produce.

Have thoughts which are uplifting. Take actions each and every day that affirm the belief that good is coming to you. Take the following statement to heart:

Every day in every way my life gets better and better.

Seeing is doing. When you see a brighter future, then your future is brighter. If you're having a hard time right now, take heart. The clouds will part immediately and the sun will shine through. Remember, no matter how bleak life looks in your here and now, above the clouds the sun does shine. It may be winter now, but spring is right around the corner.

The World is a Feast.

Help Yourself!

You are a wonderful person.

You are Unlimited.

Second SERIES BOOK-2-
You Are Unlimited©

(Your Unconscious Forces and How to Use Them)

Your conscious mind is a small part of your overall mind. These secret principles now revealed show you how to program your mind to create riches, success, and love beyond your wildest dreams. <u>You can do it</u>! This secret knowledge makes you an unstoppable force able to attain whatever you desire.

We guarantee it!

If you use this book for 30 days and are not 100% satisfied we'll refund your money. You have nothing to lose, and everything to gain. . . <u>and we mean EVERYTHING!</u>

You will contact and command mysterious forces within you which the average person doesn't understand and can't use. Success and power . . . is guaranteed! If you use this book for 30 days and aren't completely satisfied, we refund your money.   Regular price: $9.99.

Special limited offer: only with this offer and only available to people who have read **The World's a Feast.** Clip this coupon and order now and we'll take %10 off the price.

You Are Unlimited	$	9.99
(66 pages) less 10%	-	.99

Discount price	$	9.00

NAME _____

ADDRESS _____

_____
                                                        zip

Credit card number _____-_____-_____-_____

                                                 Exp date _____

Send check or money order to: **Wisdomgame 17230 Rayen St. Northridge, CA 91325**

Use this coupon special offer to be unlimited.

YOU ARE UNLIMITED!

We want to hear from you. Please send us a letter or a note.
WISDOMGAME
17230 Rayen St.
Northridge, CA 91325
Or
Webmaster@Wisdomgame.org

THIRD SERIES -3-
PROJECT MANUAL TO BRING HEAVEN TO EARTH©

Do you have a screenplay, novel, invention, house remodel, or art project, but you can't get it done? Do you have a product you want to make real? Want to make money from your ideas? This easy 30 day program develops your creativity and brings your ideas into reality. Use the step by step process in this workbook for one month and <u>you will finish your project!</u>

WE GUARANTEE IT!

If you use this book for 30 days and are not 100% satisfied, we'll refund your money. <u>You have nothing to lose.</u>

This manual brings Heaven to Your Earth. Your project can produce money, joy, friendship, and happiness and bring you the objects you desire, but it's not doing you any good sitting in the drawer or on the drawing board. You have to finish it!
It's easier than you think. In a simple, straight-forward way, using your natural creativity, we guide you in the process of making your project real. If you don't yet have a project, in 30 days you will have one, and it will be real. GUARANTEED!
Special Limited Offer: Only to readers of The World's a Feast . . . .
. . . . take 10% off the price.

MANUAL TO BRING HEAVEN TO EARTH	. . . .	$ 32.99
(200 pages)	Less 10%	- 3.30

		$ 29.69

Credit Card Number _____-_____-_____-_____

Expiration date _____

NAME _____

ADDRESS _____

_____
                                                                                    zip

Or send check or money order to :
   Wisdomgame
   17230 Rayen St. , Northridge, CA 91325

Thank you!

You __are__ a wonderful person.

__You__ deserve all the world has to offer.

You __can__ have it all!

THE WORLD'S A FEAST

HELP YOURSELF!©

WISDOMGAME®

----

www.ingramcontent.com/pod-product-compliance
Lightning Source LLC
Chambersburg PA
CBHW080553090426
42735CB00016B/3228